FLYING TAKES A COMMITMENT FROM THE WHOLE BODY

JESSE WILLIAM OLSON

For Rachel, my parents, the Schaumburg School of Poetry[1], and all who
- supported me in this endeavor by listening politely and laughing occasionally when I read my work
- let me rant about rhyme or metaphor or center alignment
- joined me in shouting about stuff online, and who made me feel a sense of literary community in my life.

Also for my students, past and future, as well as my teachers, past and future. Writing is often done alone in silence, but at its core it is an act of communication and empathy, making connections across years, generations, and all else that divides us.

---

[1] The first and (so far) only rule of the Schaumburg School of Poetry--which meets each Wednesday at a local cafe--is that the word "grey" is always to be spelled with an 'e' unless you have a very good reason not to.

CONTENTS

INSTRUCTIONS FOR USE

1. Fold back the cover of this book on both sides so as to reveal the pages.

2. Remove the pages from the book as close to the spine as possible. Recommended implements for this task include a chainsaw or a flamethrower.

3. Set the spine + cover combination aside for a moment.

4. Deal with the pages in whatever way you see fit: Suggestions:
   a. Throw them into the sea.
   b. Hand them to strangers at the local supermarket.
   c. Pin them to a favorite tree in the nearest forest.
   d. Eat them[2].

5. Retrieve the spine + cover combination and fold it like a simple paper airplane. Congratulations! You have achieved a simple suboptimal flying device. Tie a string to it, throw it, and see where it takes you.

---

[2] While some readers have reported the consumption of the pages contained herein to be particularly useful in treating various minor ailments such as hiccups and jet lag, these claims have neither been investigated nor confirmed by the FDA. Proceed at your own risk.

CIRCLES

If you fall forward fast enough,
the ground cannot catch you;
we call this orbit.

Just as the Earth falls toward the Sun
or the Moon falls toward the Earth,
we fall toward despair.

But ditch carry-on baggage like
previous intentions or politics or sleep or
doubts about how important you are, just
hold your wings out, go like mad, never stop,
and you'll never crash;

we call this "Not much. I'm fine. You?"

I WISH

I wish all screens would shatter
and we'd see through to the path before our feet

I wish all cars would crumble to fertile earth
and tires change to giant seeds of trees
with arms like Atlas, lifting up the sky,
and roots like ancient wyrms
buckling asphalt.

I wish all skins and pretenses were shed like gloves
and bare hands shaped clay and cupped water
while our feet gained foothold in the sky.

I wish the wings I spread would lift me,
do more than cast deep shade.

Flying takes a commitment from the whole body.

WHEN THE FLOOD CAME

We weren't the first to notice.
        More water in the gutters, sure,
        and Prospect Park was generally more damp,
        but we were inland, like Broadway,
        where they kept the plays running
(at first)
even as the ocean found handholds, and
        having swallowed docks, breached
        the fabled streets of New York
        with unbridled curiosity.

But what's some water in the street?
        Or exploring basements, which,
        when we tired of pumping out
to the inflooding streetflow, we abandoned,
        moving into each other's upstairs apartments
        while bridges fell and tunnels and subways flooded,
exits cut off. We talked
how crazy this would be to look back on one day

like the people of Pompeii must have
when Vesuvius first shivered.

When the flood came,

        my reflection rippled against my feet,

        and I felt hands upon my shoulders.

        It rose, but I didn't,

        having rooted myself

to the things around me.

When my body had drowned

        and I met my reflection face to face

        I, roots clinging, soggy, and rotten,

at last noticed the taste of air,

considered how candles burned, and

wondered about fish

or well-draining soil.

HAVING WRITTEN A GOLEM INTO A STORY

"It's certainly a creative story, but-" she begins
and I smile, ink ready like Sisyphus's boulder,
"-since you've named the creature-thing, he needs a gender."
My pen clatters against the table.
"But it's a lump of clay given life by a magician!" I argue.
The critique group is hushed, not taking sides.
"It doesn't have a gender."
"Yes, well,
but you've humanized him.
Made him the main character."
At this, like a hiccup, the scene freezes.
A barista's hand extends untaken change;
a newspaper reader's elbow has bumped a spilling coffee; etc.
"Yes," I intend to say, "I did," or
"that is rather the point of things here," or
"no, I brought it to life, but I did not humanize it,
it dwells well beyond human perspective," but
before I rise, flip the desk, and mic drop, the world realigns
and I cough. "But he literally has no genitals."
I blurt this to the woman twice my age.
"Aha!" she cries, pointing pen click-end like a spotlight.
And I feel guilty for suggesting genitals even matter
before realizing the pronoun I'd used.

"No," I should have said,

"my slip-up isn't proof that it needs a gender.

It's evidence that language

can tether us from rising to our potential,

that language limits us like fences keep us from exploring,

that doors closed for too long begin to resemble walls."

INK & ASH

the strands of her hair

blow off in the breeze to cobwebs like

the last dandelions, dry and blown bald ages ago

and anger or fear rises to her shoulders

      immolation

up the needles of a dead pine

      rats

up the mast of a ship

whose course plotted rocks ages ago

now the roots that crawl from her toes

      uproot

and the branches in her arms

      outstretch

and the tidal swell of dust and detritus she leads

from her lonely island in the night

rolls on the wings of a thousand flies

that roil and hiss

an old song

written ages ago in wisps

of ink and ash

DOWN

teacher says raise your hand if you need help
and, heads down, everyone busies themselves at lonely desks
like we don't all need some help

then the sun, off its kilter, tumbles
into a snowbank & fizzles out

so I throw both hands skyward,
        stand, and yell

but the teacher alone looks up at me like
        no, that's just a thing people say
        no one can actually help you
        sit down, son
        lower your hands

and he pulls shades
        then points at the desk before me

"shame about the sun," someone mumbles

MISRUNG

Blank paper rises—an unscalable wall
across the path of my perfect poem.

The blood in my fingertips brushes a beautiful truth,
which my alphabet fails to hold.

I would climb a ladder, could I build it strong,
of pencil stubs and broken lines
and all that I do wrong.

BETWEEN DARK TREES

we approach problems rationally
striding across generations
from a fire sunset to the dark arbor of night
with selfless hands outstretched
with fully open ears
while our flaws and failings flicker like lightning bugs
among the evening forest,
bright sparks, all noted, measured, predicted

though we know enough not to chase such wisps
blindly, between dark trees, where we would lose ourselves

instead, we gather them in lanterns for those who follow
and set them behind, beside the gravel path
which we build purposefully
pebble by pebble

ON DEPRESSION

One of those Tolkien forests you can never leave,
each day a tangle of snaring roots and
shifting paths, dizzying you into circles, hinting lights
and laughter echoing in your peripheral
but wisping up in ash and shadow when you look directly,
leaving you collapsed on the damp moss in a blue fog
by a poison slime river you're half minded to fall into,
with only the spiders of anxiety to converse with,

but you'll fight or wait or
inevitably somehow
leave that depression and, by the forest's edge,
the straight-lined sun and ready oxygen will ignite
on the spark you kept forgotten
deep in your lungs, somewhere,
then you'll turn and scream fire,
not flickering matchstick pleasure,
but forest fire of deep-root scorched-earth fresh-baked joy
as the late shadows torrent into charcoal smoke
beneath an infinite sky.

ON SHADOWS

Umbra means "shadow" in Latin,
so with a diminutive suffix, umbrella means "little shadow,"
because even though we'd all be dead without the sun

sometimes you need to carry your personal darkness around.
And that's fine. Your reasons can be your own.

We are not beings of starlight, because,
like candle flames, such creatures wouldn't cast their own shadows
or get bullshit skin cancer.

ON SOCIAL GATHERINGS

other guests swim in packs and "make conversation"
a quick give and take, a sea of voices shuffling
like cards in a deck

beyond, watching wide-eyed,
our protagonist bubbles out occasional syllables
which float up unanswered,
lonely barnacles clustered at the ceiling

ON STREET PREACHING

"AND SO THE SIGNS ARE CLEAR: THE WARS, THE SINS, THE INGRATITUDE OF EACH NEW GENERATION. AS IT WAS FORETOLD, I TELL YOU NOW THERE WILL BE A RECKONING! THE END OF DAYS IS NIGH AND—"

You try to look away in time, but he notices that you've noticed him.

"You there!" he looks you up and down, but does not acknowledge that you're inexplicably dressed in medieval clothing and armor in the middle of this sunny Sunday on State Street. It's Madison, after all, and who is he to judge?

"Hello brother!" you say, offering him one of the plums you purchased on discount from the fruit stand because it was almost beyond ripe. "I like what you are doing. Way to engage with the world. We need more of this sort of thing. May I?"

And as he bites into the plum, you raise the megaphone he'd set on the blue newspaper stand beside him, and you shout:

"DENIZENS OF THE CITY! WHERE ARE YOUR DOGS? THEY BARK FROM THE WINDOWS, THEY ANXIOUSLY

GNAW AT THEIR BONES, THEY LONG TO WALK
BESIDE YOU, TO FEEL THE BREEZE FLAPPING THEIR
FLOPPY EARS, BUT DO YOU HEED THEIR JEALOUS
CRIES? NAY, YOU'VE FETTERED THEM WITHIN Y—"

But he manages to snatch the megaphone back and you figure it's
about time to move on.

RAIN IN THE DISTANCE

you hear rain in the distance
is this your last night in the world?

winds shift canvas flaps; ropes creak
the horn sounded long ago, you knew
what this was when your sisters and brothers fell
before you
that sun has fled and now
you hear rain in the distance

the squirrels have filled full their notebooks
as your ears fill with shadows
which no longer see the music of the mead hall
as branches take their turn at the song
playing a goblin lyre, unstrung
still uncarved from the tree
still living, an elfin thing
roots thirsting in the field you once knew
and something ancient sings in your veins

the horn sounded long ago; we knew what this was

when grass took root in the castle

abandoned by kings filled with wine

how would you like to do this?

we know the endgame here

there's a reason you decorate the camp with bones

ON WINTER

We celebrate summer harvests when life lounges eternal
and we fall back on hills of fern or clover
to look back through the spiral arm of our galaxy
and wonder at its center
as nearby drums and dancing and cheer
follow on toward dawn

but we celebrate on the darkest nights of winter, too
thankful for the warm comfort of woodsmoke
good blankets, family, and song,
huddled and awake with the knowledge that
some of us may not make next summer's harvest

but we celebrate anyway,
because what else can we do?
Life is still ours, our time in this middle place is a gift,
and gifts are for sharing.

SALVAGE

The morning flitters away
        like you dropped a basket
    of those helicopter seed pods
        into (accidentally) an intersection
and there's a gust of wind;
    you can't possibly pick them all
        back up
cars are crunching and snapping greedily over and by
        —backing up over to crunch them again—
    and your empty basket is like an empty bowl
    reminding that you forgot to have breakfast.

    Why did you gather those anyway?
    (your brain knew each one from each one)
    You know people don't find purpose in them.
    (hands clutch several salvaged broken seed pods)
    Just get a real job. Quit this.
    (stash them in the basket!) (quick!) (gather more!)

SENTENCES LIKE GNATS

Sentences like gnats swarm your face,
some similes, some imagery, or slant rhyme,
harassing you. Demanding attention.

You swing, furious
       to put one in its place,

but each attempt at
       "Stay there. Be still!"
     ends in dead blood
         and spare wings

squished across paper;
      only a broken beauty

and blame smearing clumsy fingers.

WHY DO I WRITE

Because stories are the soil, pregnant and teeming,
in which lives take root

Because sentences, shaped and strung, are lung-filled lanterns
       glowing on the path between our houses

Because the memetic cloud snowed a dictionary's worth
       of words across my yard,

       and you're damn right I'm gonna build a snow fortress

THE PYRAMID

I don't sleep much most nights.
Acid reflux or nightmares. I eat too much.
Invisible goblins nag about the future, prod my belly,
prick at exposed toes or shoulders,
offer tastes of the figs of anxiety from their goblin merchant
baskets.

We are all given more than we can handle alone.
"Come buy, come buy!"

I roll under my heavy blanket,
curled fetal or stretched

and float headlong through the breakers
into that dark sea well-known
where we climb the pyramid we shipwreck on.
The tides swell and simmer, splash against stone, and
each step seems unsteppable, unskippable
as the spoons we draw back and fling
from the strand, raging against the eternal note.

Each level is a drowning; we form tribes like children
on the beach.

We are all given more than we can handle alone.

Longingly, the children stare to the enigmatic glow above,

a bright explosion with a corkscrew trail.

We keep arms in close, and mutter,

Why is no one pushing me up? Pulling me up?

I put my foot down.

We compare ranks on the confused plain, although

we are all given more than we can handle alone.

SCUTIGERA COLEOPTRATA

Stains on my walls, and across several magazines
are proof enough that we have met before;
yet you hound me. Why?
Have you come back to drink the blood
of your old piled corpses?

What do you eat? What do you do, but wait on my walls
waving your many—too many—silky arms, lazily taunting me,
asking what? What will I smash against you this time?
My copy of *Coraline*? The complete works of Christina Rossetti?
My soft and fleshy palm?

Villain, do you gain pleasure from this?
What is the cause of this haunting? Is it
that I live in a basement apartment?
That I did not cry at my uncle's funeral, last week?
That I did not give that vagrant change on the way home, after?

I've sent you death ten times since then!
Or do you come without a reason,
and is my mind now raising phantoms from the yellow wallpaper
of my jobless, friendless, basement solitude?
Out, out, damned spot!

Damned spot, damned maggot, damned centipede,

damned whatever-you-are that I cannot identify, because

I have found no book on insect identification

to smash against you

detailing just who or what sent you,

or what omens your splotched entrails portend.

AROUND MY HEAD IN SWARMS

A poem about tensions in the world
the girl with red bandanna & raised fist
in Pilsen Saturday—or no—a swirl
of abstract images, of snake-tongue lisped
through lines like infantry on sheets of rain
—still better yet, a sonnet on the birds
and wild of Busse, wet and yet contained;
the elk and I meet at the fence, like Earth's
last issues to negotiate. I count
three nests of swallows in this picnic shade
and still the baby skunk had flies around
its head in swarms. I watched it crawl away
—or so, are no words suited in the end
while, slowly, still, the ink dries in my pen?

THE SQUIRREL THAT LIVES IN MY PILLOW

That squirrel whom I have never seen
crawls out of my pillow at night with careful hands
     curls into a spiral in the depression
     between breast and shoulder
then whispers stories she has eaten
     in previous lives.

Lonely to be heard, to be known,
unable to be fed dreams in turn,
     she hungers
     gnaws back what she's given
     tail tip flicking my eyelids
before she retreats at dawn's light
and I awake with the crumbs.

RULES FOR POETRY

RULE 1: Start with a simile that punches stomachs
      like going the wrong way through a turnstile.
      (This is advice for writing an okay poem.)

RULE 2: As you regain footing, notice the damp grit
      of the floor. Never don't take inspiration there.
      Question each component of your worldview
      as you repack the spilled contents of your bag.

RULE 3: Discard junk that prevents adaptability.
      Are gender roles, punctuation, or politeness
      trash concepts? Ditch that shit. Be your future.

RULE 4: Forget poetry. Find life's wounds. Mind the gaps,
      then stitch bold bridges. Make doorways of walls.
      Be a passenger train that lays its own tracks, blaring
      across deserts or fields of unexamined doing.

RULE 5: When you've finished typing your poem,
      revise it, share it, save it, forget it, get it tattooed,
      et cetera. Just don't fucking center align it.

FROM A CAT SLIGHTED

It lies there, pink and pale,

    squirming in its cradle,

    writhing in glad attention.

           The Tall Ones used to call me,

used to hold me,

    stroke me,

      used to know me as Their pet.

     But this human

        thing, this worm,

           it lies shrieking,

               and what do They do?

                  They coo, They

                    coddle,

They

    cuddle and bow for it—

    I am cast down from Their favor,

    —For it? What does it know?

      I creep by silently

        and no heads turn.

          I hunt, I kill my own food—

            dead rats lie still

            proof of my tribute,

my devotion,

       left on Their doorstep,

             rotting.

It? Who has been here longer,

      who knows every corner more?

        I, I rub my paws, I set

          my jealous claws to rend.

             ...but was I practice, and

              nothing more?

I, who served my Masters well, and first?

             Who took the life given

                   and

made it shine gloriously?

Must I now bow before

     this infant man?

        This maggot will know

          whom it has supplanted.

ON POLITICS

You may think your fears
        and piles of prejudice and ignorance
        total up to useful politics
and I might suggest an alternate opinion
        in strong terms, regarding divisiveness
        or destruction vs. functioning empathy
                while testifying that my family extends far, far
                beyond my bloodline or way of seeing the world

but I forget, sometimes, that
we both have to deal with hiccups
or runny noses, and the cold air.

A LINGERING NOTION AFTER HAVING BEEN SHOT DEAD TRESPASSING

We saw the earth once, changing in the weather,
before I died, and sat by the back door
as brothers watching Fall leaves fall together—
first one, then two, then ten, then hundreds more.
You called them secret letters in the wind,
each one a message sent out to the world
and posted by a quiet death, then pinned
upon each doorstep, in the gutters swirled.
At last they land, and lay, and wither rotten
underneath men's boots and winter's snow,
the unread reams of papers piled forgotten,
never to be back in winds that blow.
I understand this now, but still believe:
Life is not the tragedy you grieve.

It was a childish day, a sunlit boy
who crossed that boundary where now shadows dwell,
in search of mischief, thinking to annoy
a lonely widow's peace. Her words would tell
no thing, but nonetheless I saw the way
the years had driven rivets through her pain
to keep in peace her heart, to keep at bay

what thing lurked in the corners of her brain.
I laughed first when with spider hands she spun
fears into substance on the spot, and turned
her eyes on me. But when I saw the gun,
I stopped. Saw her soul as the bullet burned
its tunnel through my head. I hit the ground.
She saw what she had done and made no sound.

The ghost of a lost child hovers round
half-rinsed-off dishes in the place my veined
blood emptied to her floorboards with the sound
of aching death. Just barely she regained
her life, and now she lingers, unconfessed,
and makes her mundane way while permanence
falls home. Still no one knows just where I rest.
The house is guarded by a calm white fence
with white grasshoppers peeling in the paint,
erected after neighbors flocked and stared
and shouted, first, then whispered—until faint
lost shrugs and nods were all anyone shared.
That house still bears her life, still knows with silent
walls what happened, and where all my years went.

So having lost me, you took others in
your flock to teach and raise them safe, to keep
them watched, to keep them from mischance. The sin
of God, dead skins of children in the deep

of time, you thought to stop? But think of me,
my brother, like the dying of the fall
as seasons change to a dark shifting sea
of snow and ice, but rise then after all
through buds and streams and sunlight in the spring.
Larval things take sustenance from lives
Fall drained to fertile dirt. These spillings bring
no harm into the circle, death deprives
life of no beauty. Hear me as you're tending
to the flock: there is no sin in ending.

You've let this notion linger on, that things
may be, or may not be—as if all years
sheer from us, like a reaper's blade that swings
at each forgetting, memories and peers.
But brother, time will flow whether you fight
to catch each leaf that sinks into the stream
or if you let some go. The difference, right
until the end, is just how much you seem
to struggle. All that we leave lingers too,
with truth, with love, with life: it is not lost.
Be brave at last, let go, and journey through
your world with ready eyes, arms open tossed.
Don't weigh yourself with burdens from the past;
these things are lifted—cleared—and rest at last.

A daily purchase at the general store

"so that'll be two dollars, thirty cents,"
the cashier nods, slinging out the drawer
with a slump of change. From the school fence
you watch her errands until recess ends,
and count heads as they come in one by one
while she steps singly by the school. It sends
the wrong impression, some say, what is done
has passed. Life should not be kept in tow,
choked while ancience waits to snare and wither.
All have served their purpose even though
you felt it badly. Brother please: forgive her.
Old ferns of maidenhair about the mound—
not red, but green—grow soft where I sleep sound.

AMONG THE LINES

You quote line numbers and pages and I feel
splayed out between glass panes.

You turn pages
like you dissect me. Stop.

Close the book. No,
close yourself in the book.

Feel my paper skin fold you in
the paragraphs of my arms.

Drink ink to blood. Smell my beating heart
behind each word.

Cover yourself with me.
Be bound by this binding.

Trip down between the lines,
and linger on this sentence.

AN ECOSYSTEM OF PLACES

Sun crests the hill at Ohiopyle
—they call them mountains here? I think—
bags are returned to the car; the cabin once
again womb-like, waiting.
Frost melts to diamond glitter on the deck,
drips in tears down the car-top
carrier.
A restless schnauzer eyes us anxiously
pads her front paws back and forth
watching the slow pack.

The world is larger than I can comprehend:
it is an ecosystem of places and habitats.

I choose which spaces I inhabit,
often poorly, often
from routine
often white windowless walls
which don't present the view of water
trickling down a gully
among dead fall's leaves. Often
walls unenriched by woodsmoke
or a beginner's fiddle.

FINGERS LIKE ROOTS

Fingers grip earth like roots move rocks
as I dig a basin for ablution
to plant, like a secret capsule, my mind
to blossom into whatever forms
grow from this soil.

I will cover it with a blanket of pebbles and loam,
a carpet, sunbaked warm,
and I will wait barefoot above, dogcurled and basking.

It's a risk, of course.
Like airplanes, or any germination.

LIGHT SWITCH

The library at my school started getting rid of books
because sometimes you just need to throw things away.

Among them: one entire history of the 20th century
           one month per page.
cover the size of a laptop screen
thick as the space between your headphones
and heavy as twenty-five Samsung Note 7s
           (tons of firepower there)

While I write this ISIS is destroying ruins in Iraq;
temples of previous peoples pulled to rubble
like a library cleaning its shelves,
like a salamander cauterizing memorizes
two men in the night stomach-pumping the waste
because what good is something that just sits

                              and takes up space?

There's no saying relevant to throwing out history books.
As a student once asked:
"What's ONE example even of people
who were doomed to repeat some terrible historical event
just because the world forgot about it?"

He couldn't think of any.

The world is a McDonald's ball pit
and we're all schoolyard victims and bullies in one.
Blood peeking out at split lips and knuckles, a hesitant vitality,
unsure whom was beating on who, or whether it ever went

the other way.

In the age of the meme:
Success Book:
- was going to be thrown out
- rescued by an English teacher

Good Guy English Teacher:
- rescues book
- even writes a poem about it!
Confession Bear:
- sometimes I make a bunch of references to books and pretend
my poem is deep while actually just writing cliche stuff about
society these days and whining pompously about non-issues
because maybe I lack true depth, and... this only slightly bothers
me.

But I am Fraa Jad singing my way through reality;
staring into time and turning through,
page by page,
month by month,

one hundred years collected in this heavy book.
And as Fraa Jad says, topography is destiny,

so if form follows function,
this book is a brick best built to bludgeon.
Swipe left. Swipe left.
What point is there in heft?
Throw this tinder on the fire
and like an island full of boys
we can paint our pixel masks
while we revel in the glow,
because nobody needs books anymore.

The pig skull inside us all grins as
our skeleton arms lift up their spears.

But oh, the girl with seashell ears and eyes like glassy moons,
she has no verb in her sentence. Oh, oh Mildred.
Guy Montag subjects her to poetry in the room that
never had a fourth wall.
He stares as she stares at the object and twitches her foot
and the salamander licks its lips.

Click here to discover Fahrenheit.com's shocking truth:
451 reasons why there is no use
to things that just sit and take up space!
This place is Lit, folks.

But does this even-handed justice commend the ingredients
of our poison'd chalice to our own lips?
Like human, like face, like unopened book.
(I write this glass-eyed, reclined, ear-shelled, shade-pulled, bathed in
Facebook screen-glow)
Because nobody reads books anymore.

But I saved this one history book from the trash:
Reader, I took it home.
(After sagging my shelf for two years, it was given to a friend.)

The world is a dim daycare playroom and all the people
merely children
punching blindly;
Flipping each other off in the dark
with fingers that should be flipping the light switch.

OCEANS OF ACCOMPLISHMENT

You scratch your story red upon the world,
and, puerile, claim old Nike for your bride
as though she were a thing to be attained
or tamed by such as you, who, unconstrained
by wisdom's sage advice, let nascent pride
paint lust across the flag you have unfurled.

But look beneath: this life's a palimpsest
with other stories cut under your spree.
Once other hands built taller towers here,
and layers patch on layers written clear
in stacks from Nike's footfall to her knee.
As she wades on, you draft behind the rest.

Although the surface seems to you the peak,
this is a sea. And flags as sails are weak.

STRANGER

but it's a comparative adjective, right?
"more strange," like it's a competition
trying to sort out who we shift away from in crowds
and who we make sympathetic eye contact with

and taking the six train north to central park,
when the AC water drained on us from the roof
as we rounded curves, we banded together
keeping the spot open, warning new boarders
with eyes or small hand gestures

or when it was closed southbound at our stop
and the signs were no help
and the help was stationed outside the turnstiles
the german couple and the old lady with the blue hat and I
banded together and for the next twenty minutes
no one asked me why I had facepaint,
a knee-length tunic, a shield, or a bag of foam swords

but a mom apologized that her toddler liked guitar
and wouldn't stop reaching for my lyre
and making noises
so I played it, although the train made it hard to hear

and the man in line at McDonald's, February in Chicago,
talking to himself that it's gonna get hot, mid 80s, even 90s
holding a box fan at his side, cheap wine fumes
curling around his vowels, but I ask him what, here? now?
and he blinks home and says no, it'll be slower than that.
Not until May, and is this the line to order?

And I know these people, simplified, labeled, stripped
to their minimum surface traits
(matching shape to hole, we drop the wooden blocks)

maybe
we're all kinda familiar
regardless

PLACES YOU GO

insane isn't a place you go
when the obligations of life come criminal to collect
like thugs, fists dumb as hammers, and you realize they've blocked
off all exits

when the weight of adulthood you've gained strains weak limbs
and you're sinking—gasping above water on weekends,
but mostly hiding and holding your breath
beneath the surface where none can see

when, despite the metaphor that keeps you floating,
life would rather see your "not waving but drowning" routine
from a different perspective—your gasping head
is a mole in the eternal watery whack-a-mole massacre
and your obligations are a spoiled child on a parent-paid spree
in the arcade

insanity is not a descent beneath the waves
it's a forgetting
of the strings of the puppeteers
of their whack-a-mole hammers
it's a forgetting
that you can't breathe water

that this isn't home
it's the realization
that you've always breathed water so why worry?
it's a lifting,
an elating,
a transcending
and the choking waves are the weaving fingers of your caressing
mother

and you are a child, cared for and curled

the ocean isn't a place you go
so what the hell were you doing in the water?

TO A POEM THAT I MET IN THE SHOWER

I was attacked by a poem last week,
while I was in the shower,
it begging, write me, write me!
and me all, no, I'm in the shower, get out.

Honestly, I explained, when it came again later,
when I was decently wrapped in a towel,
I'm not much of a poet.
And I didn't tell it to its face, but I also didn't think it was
much of a poem,
so I wasn't sure what good would come
to either of us from such a pairing.

But it insisted, and I agreed to try and the poem came to me
and it said,

Writing is like having mashed potatoes in your shoe.
You've just got to overcome your fears
and step into it, feeling the buttery words blend around
the imprint you leave
mashing out the gritty details between each toe
starchy thoughts overflowing the edges, salt and pepper creativity
exploding like a bad metaphor

that you don't really want to deal with even though it secretly
excites you
when you finally get your foot down firmly to the sole of things.
Writing is like—

Hey, um... poem? I said. This is not working.
I think we need to break it off. It's done, over, I should never have
tried to be a poet.

It, uh, it just disappeared when I interrupted it, and it hasn't come
back since.

Then I felt a little bad, and I got to thinking,
hey, we're both just getting started, right?
Maybe I was a little too harsh?

Anyway so, poem, if you're out there:
I just want you to know that I'm willing to give it another try,
even if we're both kinda new at this.

Y=1/X

Before the angel came it witnessed
two pillows on a bed,
one folded halfways, squished sideways, ruffled
a pile of sheet and quilt, a spent cocoon,
half hanging to the floor,
half covering half the legs of half the relationship
and no late night sounds in the other room.

Before the angel came it witnessed
one wayworn pair of sandals,
still memory molded to wake-time imprints,
slowly shedding leather skin like crinkled leaves,
lonesomely watching the hall by night,
holding down the home from dream drifting,
bound with dirt.

Before the angel came it witnessed
no more meat in the fridge,
in the cans on the shelves,
in the drawers,
in the freezer,
a poor man's vegetarian diet, cutting back, simpling,
huddled over the cabinets like an Egyptian plague.

Before the angel came it witnessed,

an hour earlier, silhouetted in his nightmate computer screen,

a pixelglow of fairies washing over unwashed cobweb hair,

tied back like the tangled emissaries

of mouse, keyboard, power,

of unknowns, the final knot.

Before the angel came it witnessed time,

between the clockhand clicks

pounded flat, hour by day by year

by the rest of life

by every drop of time

by the final stretching pause.

ART IN THE NIGHTTIME AFTER POLITICS

You and I, in this small space
encornered in the earth, we trace
designs, interweave lines, and face
the world in steady pace.

We weave knots with fingers fast
which trust our cobweb world to last
until all wind is gone and past
and emptied in the vast.

With outward eyes we'll watch men's crimes
while, backed behind by woven rhymes,
our love, two souls, elated, climbs,
ensphered in candled night.

VOYAGERS

I don't know about miles or kilometers
but I believe, with the satisfaction of adventure,

in the places left upstream,

the ground pushed by, by footfall or wheel,
history and movement, like a spun globe hurled through space;

it's what we were born with.

THE QUESTIONS THAT MATTER

Were pirates the biker gangs of the sea?

When gold dried up, did they trade sails for chrome
and chase horizon over pavement for other treasures?

Do I live in a Disney-like fantasy world
with no understanding of real bikers or real pirates?

AS WE SIT HERE

Boredom is laziness and a dulling, so I didn't know
what I wanted to do, just that I wanted something,
while life ticked by on the wall,

and I lay down on the floor and I thought
about all the things that I didn't do, all the unchosen choices,
all the missed opportunities. And I realized that

as we sit, as we stand, as we be in this place
where time drips from the edges of hours erased
to form in our soul where we feel the sublime
weight of that water washing our mind,

things are lost.

How many minutes of hours of days
have we let slip through the years in our myriad ways?
How many seconds? So,

gather your papers and plans for this life,
hold on to your backpack and run, in this life,
go somewhere. Do something. But

go, with that wave in your soul in your mind
swallowing memories, swallowing—

in life,
things are lost.

Twenty-eight seconds ago I said "sublime,"
but its meaning is water my bare hands can't pick up.
Ten seconds later I said "myriad ways,"

We choose from options:
tomorrow at 12:04 in room 110 I will tell Kelsey to stop texting,
and Zachary will crumple my voice with the thin blue lines of his
paper,
and throw my ideas, my feedback, into the trash, but
he will miss...

and I will try to teach my students that mythologies are truth
mythology is truth for those who believe
and the truth is irrelevant, claiming only one option.

And I will remember back to Thursday November 20th of 2008
when I lay on the wooden floor surrounded by candles,
and I wrote these words first in a dark blue scrawl,
while the landlordman grinned, cheating us out of heat,
and I will remember that day in 10th grade when I was driving
and I remember that day in 7th grade in the shower,

and that day in fourth grade on the bus, one third of the way back
on the right hand side with my black beaten up backpack on those
brown seats,
ripped and patched textured like pretend leather, and we were
coming along that curve on Gillem road,
it was fall, and I watched the bushes, the half-fallen farm buildings,
the four-wheeler trails, the clouds drifting, and I proclaimed to
myself
for the first time, for no reason at all, "I WILL REMEMBER
THIS MOMENT FOREVER,"
and so far I have.

But while I hold that with me, even today, I will also know that

things arc lost
as we sit, as we stand, as we sleep in this place
where we do and redo the details commonplace
everyday, and every day lose with no thought
the seconds for living and doing we sought,

and things...

Do what you are doing.
Know the details.
Notice.
Brush your teeth left-handed, maybe, or
just try having a headache, and

try being just cold, and feeling it,

try it without shoes this time, and

try singing out loud to him, and

try giving her a massage when she's stressed,

try not speaking when spoken to, try listening

when spoken to,

and

try looking us in the eyes.

And smiling

and knowing it.

CAMPFIRE

Here, but here upon this bank and shoal of time
      let's build a campfire and
twiddle our bare toes in the sand a bit.
While life lies wide before us, let's set aside
      what's done, what's undone
      and what we stress to have to do.
Here, today, now,
      let's watch the candles burn
          across the heavens,
          a spot we can't remove,
      then fall and
      bask in the dun shroud of night,
      and light our lives toward new tomorrows and tomorrows,
      be they lesser or greater,
      happier or yet less happy,
         and tonight:
            s'mores
           & warmth.

NOTHINGS

tired drips inward
like the softly pawed
come crawling homeward to hibernate

outer dims

and cloudy
falls to pillow

an exhausted

a trying

then closed and unseeing
lightless arrives
an azure oceanic
to sleep, to dream
to explore

COMMITMENT

The boy got out of bed as a squirrel the next day
shed concepts like "adult" and "job"
      like clothes grown old,
      too tight around the waist.

He ran rooftops north,
      past chimney brick
      and groggy commuter

until houses gave way to fields
      gave way to trees
      gave way

to an empty place
      filled with a single moment
      where he flicked his feather tail
      pressed paw prints in the snow
      and curled to sleep with the baking sun.

WINTER BREAK

but you realize you've become
  the pile of dirty clothes on your floor
so you shake yourself out,
stretch, examine, sniff,
  then crawl, tousled hair and all,
  into the washer for a spin

is the internet's fault, or
  blame screens, probably,
    just

  other people, gosh

when you come out, check that
  the shades are closed
  the door locked
  phone silent

a small place with
  carpet and
  pillows and
    pajamas

FLIGHT

Some decisions are hard.

Birds take their thirst for air bone deep,
        squish about their organs, and make sacrifices
        see: legs like hollow pencils
        see: freakish muscles defining their shape
        see: hearts that flicker through life like film through a
projector.

Someone leaves friends, family, and possessions behind
        for a post-doc position across the country.
Someone signs the loan
        for their new restaurant venture.
Someone quits their job,
        then picks up a notebook and a pen.

Flying takes a commitment from the whole body.

ABOUT THE AUTHOR

Jesse William Olson is a poet and speculative fiction writer, as well as a once and future teacher. He's basically from Wisconsin, though he has also lived in Arizona, Pennsylvania, Brooklyn, and the suburbs of Chicago for varying lengths of time. Hobbies and interests aside from writing include:
- Sword fighting and medieval-fantasy recreation
- Jewelry making
- Being okay-but-not-good at many musical instruments

His current favorite poets include:
- Catherynne M. Valente
- Mary Oliver
- Margaret Atwood
- Algernon Charles Swinburne
- The many spoken word artists and slam poets whose work he has voraciously consumed on YouTube, including Bianca Phipps, Rudy Francisco, Patrick Roche, and Anthony McPherson.

Photo by Rachel Worth Olson

ALSO BY JESSE WILLIAM OLSON

"Steps Ahead," a short story available on Amazon.com in the *13 Candles: Halloween Takes of Tricks & Transformation* collection from Unknown Press.

"The Lonely Barricade at Dawn," a short story available free online in the Journal of Unlikely Entomology.

"A Copy Center Journal," a short story available free online in Defenestration Magazine.

FIND JESSE AT

www.facebook.com/JesseWilliamOlsonAuthor/

or   twitter.com/jwo_writes

NOTES

The typeface used in this book is called Garamond. It's a fairly standard one. I hope you think it looks nice.

The title of this collection is inspired by a conversation that Rachel and I had while playing the *Flight* expansion for the wonderful board game *Evolution*, which was released by North Star Games. You should definitely buy it and play it.

The cover design was done solely by Jesse William Olson, though he used Rachel's camera and the GIMP image editor in the process.

Made in the USA
San Bernardino, CA
27 December 2017